Tires, Spokes, and Sprockets

A Book About Wheels and Axles

by Michael Dahl   illustrated by Denise Shea

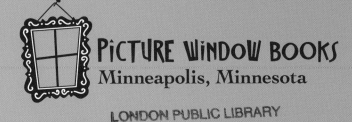

PICTURE WINDOW BOOKS
Minneapolis, Minnesota

Special thanks to our advisers for their expertise:

Youwen Xu, Professor
Department of Physics and Astronomy
Minnesota State University, Mankato, Minn.

Susan Kesselring, M.A., Literacy Educator
Rosemount–Apple Valley–Eagan (Minnesota) School District

Editor: Jacqueline Wolfe

Designer: Joseph Anderson

Page Production: Melissa Kes

Creative Director: Keith Griffin

Editorial Director: Carol Jones

The illustrations in this book were created digitally.

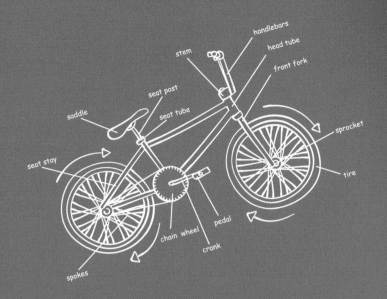

Picture Window Books

5115 Excelsior Boulevard

Suite 232

Minneapolis, MN 55416

877-845-8392

www.picturewindowbooks.com

Printed in the United States of America.

Library of Congress Cataloging-in-Publication Data

Dahl, Michael.

Tires, spokes, and sprockets : a book about wheels and axles/ by Michael Dahl ; illustrated by Denise Shea.

p. cm. — (Amazing science)

Includes bibliographical references and index.

ISBN 1-4048-1308-X (hard cover)

1. Wheels—Juvenile literature. I. Shea, Denise. II. Title. III. Series.

TJ181.5.D34 2005

621.8'11--dc22   2005024978

Table of Contents

4

Motorcycles rocket down the road. Cars zoom and big trucks rumble. Along busy streets, bicycles zip over sidewalks. Skateboards roll and glide. Wheels, wheels, wheels!

Wheels Are Machines

A wheel is a simple machine. A machine is any tool or device that helps people do work. Wheels help people move quickly from one place to another.

6